NELLY BRIMS.

# WHY MEN GO FOR RAW

*A SIMPLE GUIDE REFLECTING WHY YOU ARE BETTER A BITCH.*

# WHY MEN GO FOR RAW

**A Simple Guide Reflecting Why You Are Better A Bitch.**

**By Nelly Brims.**

**TABLE OF CONTENTS**

# INTRODUCTION

Throughout the long term, there have been different investigations on how people approach love. As indicated by traditional information, people have predominantly unique organic make-up.

By and large, it is realized that men fall head over heels for what they see while ladies go gaga for what they hear. Nonetheless, there are a few exemptions for this since certain men fall head over heels for what they hear before they start to really look at a lady's actual appearance.

This article points unequivocally to address how men fall head over heels. In any case, it is essential to remember that a portion of these focuses apply to ladies as well.

Men versus Ladies: Who becomes hopelessly enamored quicker?
Previously, the normal conviction was ladies fell head over heels quicker on the grounds that they were dared to be more personal than men. Thus, it was derived that they were probably going to fall head over heels quicker than their male partners. In any case, with late examinations, this guess has been disproved.

One of the examinations concentrating on deserving of notice is the article distributed by The Diary of Social

Brain science named: Ladies and Men in Affection Who Truly Feels It and Says It First?

This article presents an overview report from 172 understudies, uncovering that more men fell head over heels and communicated their sentiments than ladies.

In light of this exploration, ladies are bound to be more mindful while looking for a reasonable accomplice as a result of the organic distinctions between the two sexual orientations, similar to pregnancy, for example.

So a lady who needs to have youngsters would check every one of the significant boxes before she can experience passionate feelings for truly with any man.

What amount of time will it require for a man to experience passionate feelings?
The inquiry "how long does it require for a man to become hopelessly enamored?" accompanies no careful right response on the grounds that different examinations offer their response to this inquiry.

Notwithstanding, all signs highlight the way that men hang tight for a normal of between one to 90 days before they admit their sentiments. For ladies, they spend quite a while prior to letting their accomplice know that they love them.

What's the significance here to a man?

With regards to how men become hopelessly enamored with brain research, it is essential to make reference to that their interaction love contrastingly inside themselves. For instance, a few men can show their affection through activities, while others are OK with words.

Furthermore, a few men could feel butterflies in their stomachs whenever the prospect of their accomplice enters their thoughts.

While certain men can be cool headed relying upon their demeanor, additionally, at the underlying stage, numerous men don't complete an in that frame of mind into the justification for why they are enamored. Nonetheless, they are fine in the event that they see a lady they are drawn to and meet their fundamental actual necessities.

Along the line, as the relationship progresses in years, they begin to find other significant characteristics that their accomplice ought to have.

What compels a man to become hopelessly enamored certainly stands out enough to be noticed. This makes him notice his expected accomplice and inspires him to find out about them.

For the most part, men center around appearances, yet it doesn't downplay that there are different highlights that they see as engaging.

Then, they start to find out about their accomplice, similar to their side interests, likes, work-life, sexual proclivities, and the preferences, which decides whether they will adore their accomplice more or not.

Falling head over heels is a delightful and fascinating experience that many individuals don't wish to escape. It is not difficult to tell when men experience passionate feelings for ladies in light of the fact that their lives rotate around them.

The inquiry "what makes folks become hopelessly enamored?" is reliant upon a few reasons. Here are a portion of the reasons that decide how men experience passionate feelings.

1. Being acknowledged for what their identity is
At the point when a man finds that a lady acknowledges him for who he is regardless of his blemishes, he is probably going to experience passionate feelings for.

Men need ladies with whom they can have a real sense of security. They need somebody who won't utilize their inadequacies against them.

As a rule, with regards to the male brain research about adoration, being acknowledged is one of the main considerations deciding if they will fall head over heels.

A lady who is perfect at empowering a man to be his veritable self will find it simple to make him open up.

2. At the point when they are perceived for their value

Not at all like ladies, men are not ideal at translating praises from unpretentious comments. One mystery brain science to what compels a man to fall head over heels is showing him unequivocally that you perceive the truth about him.

This is additionally like causing a man to feel like he matters. To achieve this, practice it regularly to constantly help him to remember that he is so significant to the world.

At the point when he upholds you, or he gets you a gift, appreciate him monstrously.

3. Ladies who are objective driven and rousing

No man needs to experience passionate feelings for a no incredible lady plans for her life. At the point when men sense that a lady likes to be a parasite as opposed to being roused to accomplish her objectives, they will undoubtedly lose interest.

Numerous men are drawn to objective driven ladies in their profession, funds, conjugal life, and anything that equivalents making progress throughout everyday life.

Assuming you have seen questions like for what reason do folks fall head over heels so quickly, it is on the grounds that they have detected that you have shared energy, interests, and objectives.

4. A similar sexual science
One more explanation that tells how men become hopelessly enamored is the point at which they find that the lady shares their sexual science and tendencies.

One of the significant variables in grown-up connections is actual closeness. By and large, actual closeness assists with holding both the man and lady together.

With regards to the issues of sex, numerous men like on the off chance that their ladies are open and strong about it.

This would guarantee that he is drawn to the lady over the long haul since he is certain that she will be a commendable significant other.

Likewise, when the two players are not modest to discuss their sexual experiences and the preferences, it will be not difficult to have open correspondence, which connotes that the relationship is sound and bound to endure.

5. Ladies who are not put somewhere near difficult stretches
In a relationship, it is more straightforward for accomplices to face hardship together in the event that they are similar. Nonetheless, in the event that the lady

finds it trying to keep her head over the water during difficult stretches, it is a warning for most seeing someone.

To know how men experience passionate feelings, you will discover some of them posing inquiries about what they ought to expect during seasons of emergency. A man needs a lady that would give padding support as they attempt to make an exit from any issue.

In the event that a lady can demonstrate past all questions that she can be a commendable accomplice through various challenges, it will be more straightforward to get a man to experience passionate feelings for.

6. At the point when the lady is available to adore Delightful Couple Getting a charge out of Adoration Life at Kitchen Heartfelt Idea

Society is utilized to men setting the trap and ladies getting bulldozed. In any case, with regards to how men fall head over heels, it is fascinating to specify that they could do without tense ladies.

In the event that a lady is reluctant about opening up or communicating her thoughts when in adoration, the man can lose interest.

It would be hard for him to communicate his thoughts. Additionally, the man would feel befuddled and dismissed, which will make him reduce most, if not all, connection with the relationship.

7. Ladies who have a solid sense of safety in the relationship
For the most part, men would rather not be with ladies who don't feel certain and secure in the relationship. One of the characteristics that charm ladies to men is their certainty.

A lady's certainty and feeling that all is well with the world ought to be effectively recognizable to a man since it decides to a decent degree in the event that the relationship will work out or not.

At the point when a lady is sure and secure, the man will find it simple to open up and be powerless.

8. Ladies who don't battle with their ladylike side
Despite the fact that men like ladies who are positive about themselves, they actually need ladies who don't battle their female side.

Normally, one way that shows how men fall head over heels is their capacity to perform various undertakings, and they feel a debt of gratitude when their endeavors are not misjudged.

They love it when ladies open up to them when they need assistance as opposed to minding their own business.

A man will feel more sure about his capacities to be a commendable accomplice and helpmeet when the lady he is keen on isn't hesitant to impart her difficulties to him.

9. Ladies who merit constructing a future with

Actually, not all ladies have tentative arrangements for them as well as their homes in the event that they at any point need one.

Men rush to distinguish this, and when they can affirm that a lady isn't worried about her future, they will stay away.

At the point when individuals pose inquiries like what is it that a man expects from ladies, one of the normal responses is a modern driven lady.

Consequently, despite the fact that a lady is enthused about living at the time and capitalizing on it, the man should be certain that she is dealing with something more serious, particularly with her life, profession plans, and so on.

10. Ladies who satisfy their guidelines

You probably heard men utter words like "complete bundle, all out bundle, sweetheart or spouse material."

These words basically convey their aim of searching for a lady that has every one of the characteristics they need.

Despite the fact that it is very beyond the realm of possibilities so that a man might be able to see a lady that has every one of the characteristics, it is significant for them that they love somebody who meets the essential necessities as this is the means by which men experience passionate feelings for.

How does a man act when he is falling head over heels? Numerous ladies are typically worried about the mysterious brain research that compels a man to fall head over heels.

For this reason they are generally keeping watch for specific ways of behaving that men show which will inform them as to whether he is infatuated or not.

Be that as it may, in all actuality, there are no decent phases of experiencing passionate feelings for men since they act in various ways when they are enamored.

A few men can get heartfelt and keep their sentiments hidden. Others could begin parading her so that everybody might be able to see.

Furthermore, when a few men fall head over heels, they quickly get the feeling of obligation that they need to give.

The hack to decide when a man falls head over heels is the point at which he begins treating you in an exceptional manner, unique in relation to how he treats his companions, particularly females.

# CHAPTER 1

## THE STRONG WOMAN

A strong woman stands up for herself.
"She won't hesitate to share her thoughts and contemplations, paying little heed to others' thought process." "She talks about her heart and her brain." "She regards herself enough to defend herself, the causes she puts stock in, and the government assistance of others."

Some portion of a lady's right strengthening is to utilize the abilities of resilient ladies to tutor young ladies, encouraging their initiative, fearlessness, and inward strength. Without resilient ladies, the program wouldn't exist. Be that as it may, what is a resilient lady? To completely comprehend what examples we are attempting to confer on our young ladies, we should start with the starting point. What are the qualities of a tough lady?
To find the response, I accumulated the assessments of a different testing of a few resilient ladies I know. I anticipated that the responses should be definitely

unique, yet I was really glad to uncover a couple of normal subjects that went through the reactions.

1. A tough lady knows what her identity is.

"She thinks about what her identity is and what she needs for herself."

"She leans on her instinct."

"She shows her credible self and respects her senses."

Yet, this isn't static; rather, it is an always developing cycle as she investigates her inclinations. She remains consistent with her qualities as this interaction proceeds.

"She is mindful and constantly developing into her actual self."

"She develops her own advantages."

"She can comprehend and value her own assets, then utilize those qualities to make her own progress."

2. A resilient lady defends herself. This one is difficult, and requires energy and certainty, yet in addition judgment and timing. I think this is one of the main attributes for young people and young ladies to create and keep up with.

"She won't hesitate to share her thoughts and contemplations, paying little mind to others' thought process."

"She talks about her heart and her brain."

"She regards herself enough to go to bat for herself, the causes she has faith in, and the government assistance of others."

3. A resilient lady is cheerful! How is it that I could nearly disregard this one? Fortunately, I have numerous convivial and lively ladies in my day to day existence who helped me to remember the significance of being cheerful and positive.

"She brings fun into her life and anything that she does."
"She attempts to foster a feeling of equilibrium."
"She remembers her good fortune."
"She endeavors to establish a positive climate for her as well as her loved ones."
"She lives completely, cherishes hard, has a great time, and has a comical inclination."
4. A resilient lady challenges herself. Indeed, even a lady who is competent, certain, and secure in her assets should provoke herself to keep developing and pushing new limits.

"Regardless of whether life is difficult, she tries to see it as great and improve things."
"She deals with a test."
"She places one step at a time consistently."
Furthermore, she concedes she doesn't have every one of the responses. She will be adaptable and look for more data to better her life and hone her brain.

"She clarifies pressing issues."
"She has a readiness to learn, yet can be the educator when required."
"She is sure about her capacities, yet able to find out more."

Intellectually resilient ladies realize that they can claim their prosperity without sounding egotistical. They're content with their endeavors, and they won't hesitate to discuss their achievements. They're agreeable in their skin and know that they must abstain from threatening others by playing it little.

People develop mental fortitude the same way — orientation doesn't make any difference. Yet, with regards to counterproductive persistent vices that could slow your advancement or keep you stuck, orientation can assume a serious part.

My #1 book, 13 Things Intellectually Resilient Ladies Don't Do, frames the persistent vices that ladies are bound to take part in. Social tensions, cultural assumptions and the unpretentious contrasts in the ways young ladies are raised are only a couple of the variables that urge ladies to take part in these undesirable propensities. Luckily, perceiving those unfortunate propensities is the most important phase in making positive change so you can push ahead toward arriving at your most prominent potential.

Here are the 13 things intellectually tough ladies don't do:

1. They don't contrast themselves with others
Estimating your joy, riches and appearance against others channels you of mental strength. The main

individual you ought to contrast yourself with is the individual you were yesterday.

2. They don't demand flawlessness
Despite the fact that platitude, "I'm somewhat of a stickler" may feel like a respectable symbol, genuine compulsiveness will keep you down. Lay out elevated requirements for yourself while additionally tolerating that slip-ups are important for the educational experience.

3. They don't consider weakness to be a shortcoming
It takes solidarity to put yourself out there and chance being harmed. Whether you're quick to say, "I love you," or you pose an inquiry that could feel humiliating, being powerless can be the way to framing better, more joyful connections.

4. They don't let self-question prevent them from arriving at their objectives
Self-question is ordinary and you don't need to allow it to prevent you from pushing ahead. Your cerebrum will question your ability however don't completely accept all that you think.

5. They don't overthink everything
Ruminating has been connected to sadness and it can keep you from making a positive move. Participate in critical thinking yet don't permit yourself to get found out into a pattern of reasoning excessively.

6. They don't keep away from intense difficulties
Confront your apprehensions and take care of business. Challenge yourself to develop a little further consistently and you'll construct trust in your capacity to do hard things.

7. They don't fear defying the guidelines
Whether it's an unwritten rule about orientation standards, or it's a task you're not exactly equipped for, don't permit orientation standards, cultural assumptions, and rules to smother your development.

8. They don't put others down to lift themselves up
Putting others down won't land you at the highest point of the hierarchy for a really long time - you'll just keep your situation until somebody puts you down. At the point when you lift others up and turn into a real team promoter, you'll be considerably more prone to succeed.

9. They don't allow others to restrict their true capacity
Try not to let dismissal or cruel analysis stop you. You don't require every other person to trust in you as long as you put stock in yourself.

10. They don't fault themselves when something turns out badly
Recognize your way of behaving without accusing your personality. Saying, "I pursued a terrible decision" as opposed to, "I'm a terrible individual," is critical to assisting you with gaining from your slips up.

11. They don't keep quiet
Deciding not to report an episode to the specialists or not facing somebody who manhandles their power doesn't mean you're feeble — it ultimately depends on you to choose what's best for you. However, remaining quiet can deplete you of mental strength.

...perceiving those unfortunate propensities is the most vital phase in making positive change so you can push ahead toward arriving at your most prominent potential.
12. They don't regret reevaluating themselves
Whether you make a total vocation shift at age 30, or you overhaul your life at age 60, participating in self-improvement and seeking after your dreams is significant.

13. They don't make light of their prosperity
Try not to stress such a huge amount over looking haughty that you will not give yourself credit for your persistent effort and your abilities. Work on giving a straightforward, "Thank you," when you're commended and share your prosperity with others.

Construct your psychological muscle
By the day's end, constructing your psychological muscle is generally significant. Everybody can do this - - and there's generally an opportunity to get better. So work more brilliantly, not only harder, on turning into your most grounded self. Surrender the vices that are keeping you down so you can move forward toward arriving at your most prominent potential.

# CHAPTER 2

## THE INDEPENDENT WOMAN

WHO IS AN INDEPENDENT WOMAN?
However various individuals would have various impressions of who a Free Lady is or ought to be, a few portrayals would be inspected.

A lady who covers her own bills, gets her own things, and Doesn't permit a man to influence her dependability or fearlessness. A lady who upholds herself all alone completely and is pleased to have the option to do so should have been visible as being free.

An autonomous lady understands what she feels, gets out whatever she truly accepts, and lives consistent with her own qualities. She claims her own power and pays special attention to herself. She is free at all levels - she can bring in her own cash, follow her own way, and be her own closest companion. She never would require a man to feel delightful, cherished or complete. She adores herself as she is. She is of herself, of her accomplishments, of her life and of her individual however never egocentric.

How about we audit the qualities that really acquire her the title of a Free Lady.

She understands the reasonable things. She works in reality which means having the option to do various things all alone — from recording charges to effective financial planning to tracking down a decent property seller. Having the option to deal with such things assists her with being more self-powerful and gives her the certainty that she can get things going for herself. Loads of ladies don't put on the grounds that much of the time, they haven't seen their moms make it happen. In any case, she comprehends that she really wants to deliberately learn things that don't work out easily.
She tells the truth in connections. Ladies, by and large, esteem their connections to the place where they come a fairly significant distance just to get along. They are not able to express their reality assuming it disturbs another person. They profess to be what they are not so they will be preferred by their companions. This takes such a large amount of their energy and drains who they are at the center. Why bother with a relationship or a companionship where you can't be what your identity is, where you feel awkward getting out whatever you truly think? The Free Lady isn't in this way, she gets truly legit

by going up against things and looking reality in the face. She expresses out loud whatever she thinks. She states what she wants. She comprehends that her connections ought to help her, not channel her.

She defines limits at work. Ladies tend to blend feelings in with work. Subsequently, they could wind up taking on more than whatever's fair, if it's not too much trouble, individuals to a degree that hurts them and infringes on their time, lastly not getting genuinely paid for the work they do in this way parting with their power. They don't request more cash despite the fact that they realize they are being followed through on not exactly the market cost. They take care of others' responsibilities and get no kudos for it. They are gullible about interesting circumstances. They are terrified that there probably could be anything worse out there for them. With the Autonomous Lady, it is very surprising. She changes occupations to make sure she can get compensated reasonably. In the event that she understands she isn't getting credit that is appropriately hers, she sorts out ways of getting it. She shouts out when the work's hers. Finishes tasks that give her greater perceivability. She takes the necessary steps to change what is going on to incline toward her.

She deals with tracking down a solid relationship. What's preventing the typical lady from tracking down an incredible relationship? The Free lady knows she's adequate so she doesn't decide to be with men that build up that conviction. The free lady gets fair with herself about why she doesn't have the sort of relationship she truly cares about. She never considers herself to be substandard or not adorable, she never sees herself as not meriting the best. She knows her value and does things that increment her confidence. However each of this takes work and energy and responsibility, she does it to get alright with herself. What's more, I truly have a self to impart to another person. She picks who she needs to be with, the sort of man that she wouldn't be a weight to and who wouldn't control her life, yet compliant enough to address his issues that far doesn't infringe on her own life and work. She needn't bother with a man in whose shadows or triumphs she could stow away, she cherishes the spotlight being on her, yet she allows the man the opportunity to be the man where and when essential. She's available to ideas in the event that in any capacity it would be useful to her social, strict, word related and individual life.

She never moves with the group. The autonomous lady is truly extraordinary. She regards drifts yet never goes with them on the grounds that the other ladies are in it. She makes her own design, style and makes different ladies go with it as opposed to roosting on a generally imagined style. She does things not on the grounds that others do them but since she needs to and furthermore in light of the fact that she's alright with them. As a matter of fact, she's an innovator, a good example, a symbol to each and every other lady, youthful and old. Her uniqueness is apparent in design, however in carriage, appearance, discourse, disposition and individual associations with individuals.

In plain words, a free lady is rich in carriage and character, delightful on a basic level and dealing with individuals, wisely smart, appealing, exceptional, sure, mindful, straightforward, an inspiration and each and every other descriptor that could portray her individuality.

She is a certain self-inspired lady who gets a sense of ownership with her activities and never faults the remainder of the world for her missteps or her defeats. Her pride doesn't disrupt the general flow in the event that she at any point needs some assistance.

A lady, who is obstinate, inconsiderate, desolate and continuously saying that she is a free lady, necessities to quit deceiving herself and individuals around her in light of the fact that a lady needn't bother with to be bossy, or egocentric or even self-confident to be autonomous.

# CHAPTER 3

## THE CONFIDENT WOMAN

The lady with certainty figures out friendly talk and gets herself up again when emergency emerges. She puts stock in standing up once more and not offering up a social perspective to carry on with her bed life as a good example.

A certain lady is continuously safeguarding her energy. She knows her worth and her qualities and settles on choices in view of both. She's good with saying No on the off chance that it doesn't line up with her qualities and objectives. For instance, assuming she detects that specific individuals depletes her energy, she will continuously express no to spending time with them.

While some headway has without a doubt been made in orientation fairness, there is still such a hesitance to embrace the idea of a solid free lady in the work environment, in connections, and in the public eye overall.

Ladies and disgrace likewise keep on being an inescapable issue across each everyday issue. Standing up in different ways is something ladies likewise will generally battle with in light of the feeling of dread toward backfire or a pessimistic reaction.

On account of these apprehensions and the feeling of disgrace that ladies are frequently caused to feel, they will generally encounter emotional well-being side effects.

Ladies assimilate disgrace, and that might set off substance use problems. It means a lot to begin to perceive these issues in our own lives and different spots to start to stand up and battle these fundamental issues.

Men likewise assume a significant part as partners in perceiving resilient ladies and empowering their voices to be heard.

Why would that be a Feeling of dread Areas of strength toward Ladies?
While this absolutely doesn't turn out as expected no matter how you look at it, actually certain individuals stay scared or even unfortunate of solid, autonomous ladies. In any event, when a lady is positive about her power, she will in general wind up confronting hindrances in a world that stays male-overwhelmed.

Whether it's working or in connections, strength and freedom will generally lead men to scrutinize their worth and job. We live in a general public overwhelmed by the possibility of men as suppliers. Regardless of how much things have changed essentially in the last many years, a few men actually have waiting uncertainties about not being seen with a specific goal in mind.

It's trying to relinquish things imbued in your viewpoints, responses, and general way of behaving.

Not simply men are scared by tough ladies. Commonly different ladies might feel off-put by this or threatened. That might be because of their sentiments about being a lady too.

For instance, a lady might accept that different ladies ought to be calmer and blur out of the spotlight, and when they see somebody who isn't following that, they could feel like their convictions are being tested.

For what reason Don't Ladies Shout out?
While certain ladies truly do make some noise reliably working and in connections, there is a trepidation factor that keeps them from doing it for different ladies. Why would that be? There are in many cases divided worries between ladies who would rather not make some noise.

There's a feeling of dread toward being viewed as "insane" on the off chance that you make some noise or stand up. As ladies, you may subliminally see ladies who share their contemplations or thoughts as excessively forceful or close to home, so you could stay quiet to try not to be marked like that

.

At times ladies grow up discovering that they ought to be sweet and charming, and assuming you stand up on anything, you're conflicting with that.

Sadly, actually in some cases when ladies stand up on various subjects, they become the survivor of slanderous attacks. We saw that during the #MeToo development.

Ladies might be apprehensive they'll offer something wrong and be condemned more so than men. A ton of times, females hush up on the grounds that they need to safeguard themselves.

Research from the College of Cambridge found ladies are over twice less inclined to pose inquiries during a scholarly class than men. Specialists checked out at many studios in 10 nations.

At the point when ladies aren't partaking in discussions, getting clarification on pressing issues, and sharing their viewpoints, then, at that point, they aren't being addressed. For instance, there are fewer female junior researchers in numerous scholastic organizations.

## Ladies and Disgrace

A ton of what's examined above can integrate back with the idea of disgrace. Ladies frequently feel disgrace over things that a man would be caused to have a pleased outlook on, whether that is achievements working, sexuality, or being serious areas of strength for an individual.

We might cause ourselves to feel disgrace when we conflict with a normal practice we trust in, regardless of whether we understand we hold that conviction.

lady lying on the bed confronting the camera
At the point when ladies feel disgrace, it then becomes something assimilated that can make them cast their general existence in a negative light. Disgrace can prompt melancholy and low confidence, among other psychological well-being conditions.

There was a review done by specialists from the College of Toronto and Sovereigns College in Ontario. It included volunteers between the ages of 11 and 16. Those members who were bound to encounter disgrace were likewise bound to have side effects of gloom.

There's likewise a connection between being inclined to disgrace and tension problems.

There's the different, however comparable idea of culpability that can be essential for what keeps you away from depicting yourself as a solid, free lady.

The enormous contrast among disgrace and responsibility is that culpability comes from survey a particular activity adversely.

For instance, you might feel as if you've done something to another pessimistic individual and impacted them ineffectively. You assimilate this and start to feel like you're a deficient or shameful individual.

Compulsion in Ladies

At the point when you don't see yourself as a solid free lady, you might be bound to manage psychological wellness issues and substance abuse. The manner in which ladies experience enslavement can be unexpected in numerous ways in comparison to men's encounters, and treatment needs to address these distinctions.

A portion of the variables that assume a part in ladies' habit include:

Relationship issues — for instance, ladies are bound to encounter a backslide while going through issues in their marriage or when they have kid care issues.
Food and body concerns — dietary issues are oftentimes connected to substance use problems.
Confidence — numerous little kids who start utilizing medications or liquor right off the bat in their lives do as such to build their certainty.
Sexuality — numerous ladies understand that their substance use is attached to their sexuality. For instance, they could feel disgrace about the sexual maltreatment they were a survivor of, and that then, at that point, drives them to utilize substances to defeat those sensations of disgrace.

Connecting, Speaking Bits of insight, and Building Associations

So how might this affect ladies at the present time? In the first place, to turn into major areas of strength for a lady, you want to do whatever it takes to get solid regarding your psychological wellness. On the off chance that you're managing a substance use jumble, treatment is a significant stage. Try not to allow disgrace to keep you away from the consideration you want and merit.

You can not just work toward having a better relationship with yourself and liberating yourself from disgrace, yet you can likewise figure out how to talk straightforwardly and truly and fabricate associations with different ladies.

Regardless of whether you're not managing a substance use jumble, it means a lot to pursue having a solid relationship with yourself that will permit you to be more open to standing up in each part of your life.

At the point when you share your own encounters with others, it likewise helps focus a light on unavoidable issues. Ladles need to have their voices heard.

You can likewise uphold different ladies. Instead of reviewing areas of strength for a lady as bossy or tyrannical, begin to rethink your point of view. Contemplate how you feel on the off chance that a man were to act similarly. It may very well be that on the off chance that that were the situation, you would consider him to be somebody in power and meriting regard.

Shift how you view yourself and different ladies and urge others to do likewise.

Asking Why A few Ladies Appear to be so Easily Sure? lady power-and-young lady strength-in-business-accomplishment winning-and-profession achievement with-solid financial specialist pioneer in-office-raising-clench hands with-desire anticipating city-building-foundation

What is it about specific ladies that causes them to seem certain and in charge? While it might appear to be a secret — or that certain je ne sais quoi a few ladies innately have — it ends up, there are propensities that sure ladies embrace.

**How to be a confident woman**

1. Know a great deal

Certainty comes from knowing your subject matter so completely that you talk about it with complete assurance and unfaltering information. Research shows that preparation and planning for the obscure is a significant consideration in creating self-assurance. This is one of the most straightforward signs to detect in a certain lady, says Hamati.

2. Hold your head high

In any event, while you're feeling somewhat flimsy, Hamati prescribes utilizing your non-verbal communication to convey the inverse — stand upright, hold your head high, ground yourself and simply look like it.

3. Begin with little, attainable objectives
In his book Springboard: Sending off Your Own Quest for Progress, G. Richard Shell takes note of that Olympic competitors train in a manner that gathers little wins and gradually fabricates trust in their capacities. Savvy ladies can comparatively utilize this method to help certainty over the long run by putting forth little yet reachable objectives — then, at that point, expand on those victories.

4. Dress the part
Our garments can really expand our certainty when we feel better in them, notes Hamati. Ponder how you feel when you go to a prospective employee meeting in a pleasant suit. Dress for the gig you need.

5. Deal with your body and wellbeing
At the point when you feel and look great, you are more sure. The Mayo Center suggests tackling the force of your viewpoints and activities to raise your confidence — rehearsing customary taking care of oneself and defending your psychological wellness are two significant stages in building and keeping up with fearlessness, as are getting sufficient rest and exercise.

delightful young lady snoozing bed-in-morning
6. Invest more energy with other certain ladies
Encircling yourself with positive individuals can help your confidence, and thus your fearlessness. You will feel enabled around similar individuals, says Hamati.

7. Know about your environmental elements and explore the world with care
Care is a movement where you "deliberately live at the time and experience that second with every one of your faculties." When you're available and at the time, you will normally radiate certainty.

8. You do you
Sure ladies couldn't care less about marks or logos, however make their own style and tasteful, says Eileen Scully, pioneer behind The Rising Tides and creator of In the Organization of Men. Scully centers around propelling ladies in the work environment through her work and as a global featured expert; she every now and again expounds on certain ladies and she consults with ladies all around the world about administration and certainty.

9. Be energetic
Being energetic about a subject will normally build your certainty, as per Hamati. You can't be energetic and frail — the two don't go together.

10. Carry on with your life your way

Simply being blissful and partaking in your life assembles confidence and self-esteem.

11. Attempt new things
It's very engaging and energizing to evaluate the obscure, says Hamati. Whenever you've done such countless things, you will feel more certain and can examine them as a matter of fact.

12. Engage yourself regardless of what the circumstance
Hamati takes note that you ought to assume responsibility and not let others go with your choices for you — this includes in both your expert and individual lives.

13. Be brave and intense
Facing challenges is essential for being sure. As Adele says, "Be daring and dauntless to know that regardless of whether you pursue an off-base choice, you're making it for good explanation." Overcoming your feelings of dread is an exploration supported method for helping your self-assurance.

14. Say OK, yet in addition know to say no when it doesn't work for you
Saying no can some of the time be significantly more earnestly than saying OK. However, the capacity to make limits will cause you to feel pleased, particularly assuming you're great at hanging tight, as indicated by Hamati.

15. Remain positive
Simply the demonstration of being positive makes a quality of certainty.

16. Assume responsibility
With regards to your own life and maybe dating, put yourself in control and realize you're doing the picking, not the opposite way around. That mentality will provide you with a demeanor of certainty, as indicated by Hamati.

17. Lift up different ladies
Certain ladies are continuously lifting up different ladies, as indicated by Scully. Helping other people accomplish their fantasy shows you're engaged.

18. Courageously go solo
Scully finds that certain ladies can stroll into any room alone and leave with a few new colleagues.

19. Take on a development and students mentality
Sure ladies are continuously learning. They don't need to continuously talk or be the focal point of consideration. They realize they can gain significant examples from others. This counsel is upheld by research — Song Dweck found that having a "development outlook" helps individuals all the more completely arrive at their true capacity.
Take their own choices, bring in their own cash and commit their own errors, says Scully. Know the

propensities and indications of certain young ladies, and assist with imparting them in your little girls from birth — and especially after pubescence.

21. Pick your companions carefully
Similarly as you ought to encircle yourself with other sure ladies and positive individuals, Scully takes note of that certain ladies are not brought somewhere near others. Certain ladies know when to leave individuals who cut them down, without saying 'sorry'

22. Characterize your terms
Characterize yourself by your own appraisal of your value and work — don't permit others to characterize it for you.

23. Clarify some things
Concede when you don't know something, so you can learn and develop. You can't genuinely adopt a student's strategy to the world until you will concede where you need information and fill in the holes, notes Scully.

Following up: Lift your certainty (and transform you) with these 50 positive confirmations.

# CHAPTER 4

## THE BITCH IS JUST HER NATURAL SELF AND ALL INTERESTING

It's not how well you attempt to pose before a man or how tasteful you will quite often be that takes a man going off the deep end over you, probably not. It's simply that regular and novel you have been overlooking reasoning it's archaic and not OK is what he truly yearns for.

Each thought something intriguing might be preferable over obviously being great?

Clearly being pleasant to your man won't make him more committed. In her meetings with men, Argov found that men need to focus on ladies who radiate certainty and are in charge of their
Envision a world in what jobs were switched and men cooked for ladies, got socks, and couldn't hold on to get hitched. Imagine you had a beau who possessed an expectation chest with six lavender neckties inside that he believed his groomsmen should wear at the wedding. Picture him getting broken down each time you walk around a Child Hole. What's more, he welcomed you at the entryway wearing silk fighters and cattle rustler boots, so he could do a shaft dance for you. Then add a

couple of ultimatums: "Where's my ring?" "Is there any valid reason why you won't wed me?"

As terrifying as it sounds, this is exactly the methodology ladies are shown on the best way to get a spouse. It's the predicament of each "decent young lady" who puts every other person first, places her own requirements last, and doesn't think she deserves contacting the hemline of her man's jeans.

At the point when I surveyed men, they generally said certain ladies are in extremely short stockpiles. Furthermore, that sure lady is what they see as hottest. Is anyone shocked that ladies are rare? Glance around.

The typical style magazine advises ladies to behave like a worker, as though dating were a work serious, common position application: "Could you at any point serve a cool brew in junky undergarments? Do you leave dangerously sharp wrinkles in his shirts like worker of-the-month at the Sprightly Roger inn? Do you wear cellophane for him? Is it true that you are cultivating in stilettos? Is it true that you are surrendering it doggie-style? Provided that this is true, he'll drop to one knee and propose..."

Two or three gets hitched during blizzard
Several gets hitched during snowstormDavid Pyle
What ladies are gaining from this is all how to frantically act. At the point when her disposition is "Pick me! Pick me!" She raises a ruckus around town and switches on

his craving. It's human instinct. You'd be two dozen similarly as switched off by a person's roses to a first espresso date and let you know he felt like the most fortunate Wail on earth in the initial five minutes.

It's human instinct. Advising a lady to work harder to please resembles advising a young child to approach a schoolyard menace on the principal day of school and say, "Here, take my lunch cash. Also, you can have my cupcakes as well. I'll try and toss it in my lunchbox since you don't have one." Or, in a dating circumstance, "Here, take my body. What's more, I made you a cake. If it's not too much trouble, be great. If it's not too much trouble, wed me. I'll try and raise my butt quite high as they do in yoga. It's so open to being topsy . Truly. I simply love it!"

Since a man lays down with you doesn't mean he's contemplating what's to come. For him to contemplate always, there must be something he regards inside you. Like areas of strength for a... what's more, areas of strength for a.

**Relationship Standard 1**

In sentiment, there's nothing more appealing to a man than a lady who has nobility and pride in what her identity is. What's more, you need to know your own psyche. The more you center around hoisting yourself, the more he will attempt to be at the highest point of your need list. He thinks of you as a drawn out prospect when you've added the key fixing: regard. Also, regard is the magic that binds everything.

Kara is an ideal illustration of why brilliant, certain ladies dominate the competition. From the beginning, her life partner attempted to offer her his opinion on how she ought to dress. She was leaving for a gathering, and he advised her to wear a dress rather than the pantsuit she had on. Then, at that point, he told her she was wearing an excess of cosmetics. What the pleasant young lady would have done is run out and purchase another closet. Be that as it may, Kara energetically put him under tight restraints: "Tune in here, Versace. This outfit has forever been fine. Also, I haven't had any grievances about the cosmetics by the same token. However, assuming that you'd like, I'll tell you while I'm wearing this ahead of time. Like that, to see me in it, you don't need to come over."

To be taken a gander at in an unexpected way, you need to think in an unexpected way. He needs to see that you call your own shots and that you don't require input from anybody about how to put your socks on. According to this, "I'm secure." The greatest fascination of executioners is destitution and frailty. The bitch doesn't try out or attempt to be the "most incredible in show." Rather than "where's my ring" or "is there any good reason why you won't wed me," she's reasoning: "What's the upside of having this person around?" "What is my opinion about myself after I've been in his organization?" "How might this benefit me?"

And afterward something entertaining occurs: He tries way too hard to accompany her.

Kim Basinger offered something fascinating: "I lack opportunity and willpower to be named troublesome, and I lack the opportunity to mind." Men will generally feel calm with a lady who doesn't mind so much since then he doesn't need to be completely liable for another person's joy. At the point when a man sees you are content with him yet you can be similarly blissful having nothing to do with him, that is the point at which he won't have any desire to walk out on you. At the point when you are blissful, you are hot.

Single, blissful lady on her loveseat
Delightful lady perusing on a couch unwinding with her exposed feet over the arm of furniture going to give the camera a radiating grin; Shutterstock ID 155218391; PO: TODAY.comShutterstock
Not just this, bitches have some good times. My companion Angela had a date with a person on a Friday and they went out for Chinese food. They attempted a few dishes and had a lot of extras, so Angela brought back home all the doggie packs. The next night, she had a date with an alternate fellow and chose to be the "master with the mostest." She warmed the Chinese extras, "revamped" a variety on a lovely plate, and served it to her praiseworthy visitor. The fortune treat said: "The catered clamor commotion was a crushing achievement."

Obviously, I could never suggest that you pick such a fast and simple dinner over three hours of perspiring and slaving in the kitchen. Nonetheless, I would be neglectful on the off chance that I did exclude this one master connoisseur cooking tip: Don't keep the parsley. (In the event that it gets spongy in the microwave it will be blatantly obvious like clockwork.)

Notice what Kara and Angela shared for all intents and purposes: Neither one of them wanted to overcompensate. This gained some favor with the man. Why? It was normal that they take themselves out on the grounds that the rulebook says ladies should. At the point when they rejected, a light went off over his head. The message "I personally merit something" transforms him into a devotee.

In a music-channel narrative, Tim McGraw offered something extremely captivating about his significant other, Confidence Slope: "She's an honest person, that is without a doubt. She doesn't take any sh*t from anyone." He didn't decide to remark on her ability, achievement, excellence, acclaim, or any of the different things society celebrates. All things being equal, he remarked on the property men regard most: a spine. Do you believe he's pleased that his better half doesn't take B.S. resting? I'd wager that he is.

**Relationship Rule 2**

He weds the one who won't set down like tile. This carries us to the meaning of a wedding bitch — otherwise known as areas of strength for a, an exceptional lady for herself. The bitch isn't impolite or grating since she's adequately shrewd to know that being circumspect is more compelling. However, she won't think twice about seeing someone. She won't stay at work longer than required to "get a spouse." Along these lines, he doesn't characterize her as a thoughtless lady he can exploit. She has a specific spunk about her. Sugar and zest ... furthermore, not generally so pleasant — that is what lies under the surface for his fantasies.

Since many "pleasant" ladies erroneously trust that being a resilient lady (otherwise known as a bitch) is something terrible, we should investigate a portion of the models of the purported qualified lady. Then we'll determine from men their opinion on ladies who act along these lines.

Fantasy 1: You Must Be Great

Contemplate the last time you were frantically enamored. Chances are, the person was certainly not a tycoon or a mind specialist with super strong abs who was hung like a farm animal on Viagra. Chances are, he didn't get you off multiple times before he got his. In any case, something really stood out about him. He had several elements that did it for yourself and a specific wizardry that made you shiver. Men who need to fit in a relationship are searching for that equivalent sorcery.

He doesn't wed a lady who is great. He weds the one who is fascinating. This is quite possibly the greatest legend sustained by the media: In the event that you are awesome, wonderful, and rich, you will get the regard and adoration you long for. So they say. (What's more, presently back to the real world.) At the point when a man meets a woman who has all the earmarks of being unnecessarily perfect, exorbitantly sweet, or unreasonably charming, he will overall become depleted quickly.

Grandness exhibitions are a certifiable outline of how women are deceived into accepting that the principal pursuits in life are greatness tips and "man getting" capacities. In truth, they offer enlightening honors and awards, which is especially startling because the principal men watching are the ones who genuinely like blockheads. Savvy men trust it's embarrassing for a woman to stand and smile like she's reliably that shredder. Everybody understands the disappointments needed to stifle the winner, and the Southern Excellence who wins Miss Congeniality is given to tell the designated specialists: "Screw all, y'all...you revolting summabitches."

Every one of them profess to be virgins until marriage, and all are do-gooders for poor people:

Second next in line: "I'm a fifth-year junior at the neighborhood school studying stoneware. I intend to stop widespread starvation and track down a solution for malignant growth. Furthermore, for the last time, I expect to stop the worldwide lack of vases."

First next in line: "I intend to take care of the destitute, the destitute, the jobless, and the desperate. That way the entirety of my family members can eat."

Sovereign honey bee: "Before I visit neediness stricken towns in Africa, I'm fixin' to get my toes painted. Welcome the press. I'm wearing my thousand-dollar Manolo Blahnik shoes!"

In the event that you've at any point seen, magnificence shows are a ton like province fairs. The ranchers show the cows the same way. They walk their valued Jersey cow across a phase before a group of people with judges, and perhaps the cow even spins multiple times. Then the triumphant cow gets a silk strip hung over it, which has the title and the year on it. They even have year schedules including the "cow of the month."

Youthful couple running;
Youthful couple running; athletic; beau; couple; work out; female; fit; wellness; companions; sweetheart; attractive; running; way of life; male; man; nature; outside; park; individuals; rehearsing; pretty; relationship; running; sport; playful; active apparel; lively; summer; together; two; lady; youngShutterstock
So we should attempt to apply this Barbie-like way of behaving to a first date to see the reason why it goes

over like a lead expansion. Picture a lady attempting to be that "wonderful young lady." She strolls into the room like she's on a catwalk. The satchel matches the shoe button. She laughs on prompt. For supper, she arranges two olives with low-cal dressing (as an afterthought). Without acknowledging it, this lady has proactively stamped herself: impermanent. To him? "Store and go." He might have intercourse with her, yet from that point on it's a declining slide. Why?

At the point when she's counterfeit, he becomes careful about who she truly is and what her genuine inspirations are. For the most part, he calculates she's putting on an act to trap him. So it never goes to a higher level. To this end a few connections never change into second gear. By attempting to be something she's not, the lady consequently gets set apart with the "shaky" stamp. "This one will require steady consideration and nothing I give will at any point be sufficient. She'll drain me of all my energy." Before he's invested any time with her, he is intellectually on to the following.

This, yet when a man thinks a lady is powerless or unreliable, he won't want to work in the relationship. It becomes "male diversion" by then. The relationship turns into a sideshow. He'll kick back, break a lager, and think, "She's making a good attempt, I won't ever need to start to perspire in this relationship."

**Relationship Standard 4**

At the point when a lady is making a respectable attempt, a man will ordinarily test to perceive how hard she will function for it. He'll begin tossing relationship Frisbees, just to perceive how hard she'll run and how high she'll hop. Men are utilized to this. So they attempt to lure you into this way of behaving. He might let you know on a second date that he enjoys clean red toenail. Or on the other hand that he loves a specific thing of dress. Assuming you quickly start to "work" to be what he needs, it diminishes his regard.

To more readily get it, we should take a sneak look at a page inside the male rulebook. This is the secretive profoundly ordered stuff.

The meaning of extraordinarily provocative: A lady who can work all alone and deal with herself. She won't allow me generally to have the high ground. Furthermore, she can advise anybody to go leap in the lake at whatever point she feels like it.

That is the lady he'll work harder to be with. Whenever you are too stressed over another person's endorsement, that individual loses regard for you. At the point when a man sees you sneaking yourself away from the kick off, you are getting yourself in a position for an unbalanced relationship, since you support each person's implicit conviction: "In the event that you disregard her, she'll look for your approval and consolation." Endorsement turns into his as if it were "commitment." When you really want his endorsement, it blinds you and you immediately become the weak one in the relationship. Take the way of thinking of "endorsement neither wanted nor required."

Two bright young ladies, happyShutterstock
All things considered, there will continuously be somebody there to let you know that you're not adequately appealing, sufficiently wonderful, or that you didn't come from the right half of the tracks. Genuine certainty is conceived when you...

**Relationship Guideline 5**

Try not to accept everything that anybody says to you about yourself. Sophia Loren said, "Magnificence is the manner by which you feel inside, and it reflects in your eyes. It isn't something physical." This makes you lovely to a quality man, since now you show up complete. Furthermore, that makes him say, "Hmm, I wonder, what is that unique wizardry she has?"

www.ingramcontent.com/pod-product-compliance
Lightning Source LLC
LaVergne TN
LVHW020525160826
845677LV00015B/3898
* 9 7 9 8 3 6 7 3 7 9 2 3 5 *